PIONEER VALLEY EDU

ALL ABOUT
BICHONS

MICHÈLE DUFRESNE

Here is a Bichon Frise.
A Bichon is
a small, white dog.

A long time ago,
Bichons went
with sailors on boat trips.
The dogs made the sailors
feel happy on long trips.

Bichons do not get very big.
They have long, curly tails.
They have black noses
and round, black eyes.

Bichons are friendly and happy dogs. They are good dogs for families. They like to play and go for walks.

Some people think that Bichons do not shed, but they do shed some of their hair. Some people with allergies can have a Bichon.

It is good to brush
a Bichon's fur every day!
If you do not brush
a Bichon's fur,
it will get matted.

If you get a Bichon puppy, you will need to take good care of it.
You will need to give your puppy good food to eat.
You will also need to take your puppy for walks and teach your puppy to go to the bathroom outside.
If you take care of your puppy, you will have a new best friend!

TAKING CARE OF
YOUR BICHON FRISE:

O Walk your dog every day.

O Brush your dog every day.

O Give your dog fresh water
   every day.

O Give your dog healthy food
   to eat.